Tim's Garden

by Benton Walston

Target Skill Short Ii/i/
High-Frequency Words *he, for*

PEARSON

Scott
Foresman

Tim sits at the garden.

It is for bunny.

It is for worm.

It is for bird.

It is for Tim.

He likes the garden.

Tim is happy at the garden.